First paperback edition October 2020

Published by Lola & Co Publishing.
Book Illustration by Clare Thomas
Words by Gavin Clifton

ISBN 979-8-5549-1510-9 (paperback)

Gavin Clifton

MAX AND THE MAGIC WISH

MAX

BELLA

MUMMY

DADDY

ESMEE

LEO

OLD LADY

CASS

MAX AND THE MAGIC WISH

Max was born just a little different to others; his legs weren't as strong as all the other children he knew. So, he used a **wheelchair**, which had two large wheels either side, so he could wheel forward to help him get to where he wanted to go.

Max used his **wheelchair** all the time.

"**BROOM! BROOM!** HERE I COME!"

He even took it on holidays in the summer,

where he often went to the *seaside*

with Mummy, Daddy, and his two **younger**

Sisters, Bella and Esmee.

Max, Bella and Esmee were so excited

to be told by Mummy and Daddy they were

about to go away on **holiday**.

When they found out, they jumped in the air with joy.

"YES! YES! YES!"

Max stopped and began to think.

"Mummy, what about **CASS**, the dog? Can she come too?"

"**Yes, she certainly can**." Mummy replied.

"WOOF!
WOOF!"

Barked **CASS**.

"**CASS** will travel safely with us in the

boot of the car." Daddy said.

"Where are we going on our holidays?"

Esmee asked.

"To the seaside." Daddy replied.

"LET'S GO! LET'S GO! LET'S GO!"

So Max, Bella, Esmee, Mummy, Daddy and **CASS** the dog set off in the

car and head towards the seaside to start their **holidays** in the sun.

On their way and as they drove over the hill, Max could see

something blue and *sparkly* appearing out of the car window.

"What's that **bright**, **BLUE** and *sparkly* coloured thing over there?"

Max asked.

"That's the **SEA**, Max, it's where all the

FISH

SHARKS

DOLPHINS

live." Mummy Replied.

"Can we go and see all the **fish**,
sharks and **dolphins?**" asked Max.

"We certainly can." said Mummy.

THE OCEAN

9

Daddy safely parked the car up, overlooking the sparkly **bright blue sea**, and then Mummy took Max's wheelchair out of the car boot, and brought it around to the car door, and helped Max get in, whilst Daddy put **CASS THE DOG'S** lead on her, so she wouldn't run away.

"Shall we all go for a walk along the beach." Mummy said.

And all together, the rest of the family cheered a great big excited sounding

"YEEESSSSSSS".

There were lots of other families enjoying playing on the beach.

There were some families playing at the **FUN-FAIR** other

families building **HUGE** sandcastles.

And my family ready to chase crabs.

11

Daddy wanted to keep on walking along the **BEACH**, where we look for **CRABS** under rocks.

There were **SMALL** crabs,

SNAP!

BIG

crabs, **SNAP!**

12

baby crabs,
SNAP!

different coloured crabs too
SNAP!

Even **CRABS** that
DANCE!

13

As we walked along the beach, Bella all of a sudden noticed a *frail* old lady sat on her own in a beach hut. She was wearing **BIG** red shiny earrings and a purple headscarf decorated with sparkling **pearls.**

The **old lady** suddenly spots us all as we walk by and leans over to **Max** in his wheelchair and says.

"What is your name, young child?"

"I-I-I'm Max!"

"**Fear** not my little one." the old lady said.
"Why are you dressed in such funny clothes?"
Max asked her.
"Oh, these are my clothes of **wisdom**,
young man, I'm a **fortune teller**."
The old lady replied.

15

come in
let
**Mrs
Winkleton**

TELL YOUR FORTUNE

1.00

Then the old lady gets off her seat, makes her way over to the back of her beach hut, to collect a very funny **globe** looking *object*.

"What is this object you have in your hands?" **Bella asked.**

"This is my **Crystal Ball**. A very special object, an object which **never, ever judges**, an object of **promise** and **happy life**." The lady replied.

16

The **old lady** then takes Max's *hands* and places them onto her Crystal ball and then says to him,

"My **SPECIAL** one,

Please **CLOSE** your eyes,

It's time to make a **WISH!**"

7

"I **W-WISH** to be as **a-able** as all of the other *ch-children* so m-maybe I can make a new **friend.**" Max said.

19

After a **glorious** and fun packed holiday that summer with his family, Max was about to go to **PRIMARY SCHOOL** for the very **first** time. He was very nervous about starting school, because he was worried that because he was in a wheelchair, he would be seen and treated **differently** to all of the other children. Max went to school anyway, and spent his **first day** exploring.

In the LIBRARY

And in the MUSIC ROOM

20

"How was your first day at school Max?" Mummy asked.

"It was ok Mummy, but I was sitting all alone, the other children sat away from me" Max replied teary eyed.

"**YOU'LL BE OK**." Mummy said.

So Max went back to school the next day to learn new things. Then it was play-time, and all of the Children were allowed out to play in the **School yard**, including Max. All of the other children were running around and playing, but Max couldn't **PLAY** with them all, because he was confined to his wheelchair.

A few school days passed by, and every **PLAYTIME** Max would sit in his wheelchair on his own, in the yard, watching all the other children play.

But **one** day, a little boy eventually noticed Max all alone, so the little boy came over to Max and said.

"What is your name?" "M-Max" he replied

"Hello Max, my name is Leo." The boy replied.

"Why can't you walk like the rest of us?" Leo asked.

"I was born with **CEREBRAL PALSY**, which means my legs don't work the same as yours." Max replied.

"Oh, so is that why you are sat here on your own in a wheelchair?" Leo replied.

"Yes, I'm **A-AFRAID** so, and I'm worried that I **w-won't** make any friends. I also get very **nerv-ous** when I meet and talk to people for the **f-first t-time,** Max said. I worry they w-won't *understand* what I'm s-s-saying."

"DON'T WORRY Max, no need to get down; I'll be your friend." Leo replied,

"REALLY?" MAX SAID.

"Yes of course, my Mummy has told me that just because some people are a little **DIFFERENT** to others, doesn't mean they are not nice. They are just the same as the rest of us children. I will **play** with you and be your friend."

23

So for the following

days,

WEEKS,

months

ahead, Max and Leo played together **everyday**

at school, they even sat *together* causing trouble in class.

Leo, over time, got to **UNDERSTAND**, that Max needed help now and then. He'd RUN Max to his classroom ready for class. You'd often hear Max shouting.....

"FASTER LEO, FASTER, I WANT TO FLY."

Followed by

"SORRY MISS!"

26

As he was doing this, all the other children **watched** and saw how Leo and Max were becoming very **BEST FRIENDS**. They saw how Leo treated Max just the same as he treated everyone else, so they started doing the same.

If Leo was late to class,

someone else would be on hand to help Max get to class.

Now this meant, although Leo had become best friends with Max, he was also **HELPING** Max make even more friends too. The other children eventually learnt how Leo had **BEFRIENDED** Max, and did the same, meaning, Max was beginning to make lots of new friends.

Max wouldn't have dreamt of having so many friends when he first started Primary School, but now he has **LOTS,**

but he is still **WONDERING**, when his **wish**, given to him by the old lady he met at the seaside back in the summer holidays would come true?

come in let
Mrs Winkleton
TELL YOUR FORTUNE
1.00

30

So School half-term arrived, and Max's wish **STILL** hadn't come true.

So he asked his Mummy and Daddy if they could all have a day out at the seaside once again so he could go and see the **old lady** to ask when would his **wish** be granted?

come in let

Mrs
Winkleton

TELL YOUR FORTUNE

1.00

Mummy and Daddy agreed to another **family day** at the seaside,

so off on their travels they went.

Just as the whole family walked along the beach, the **old lady** spotted

them and said.

"What brings you back to my little beach hut?" special one?"

"I-I've come to a-ask you a question, miss." Max replied.

"And what question would that be? the lady said.

"Do you remember the **WISH** *that you granted me back in the*

summer?" Max asked,

"I CERTAINLY DO, AS CLEAR AS DAY." the old lady replied.

"Well, my **W-WISH** *doesn't seem to have come* tr- true *yet miss. I*

haven't become quite as a-able *as all the other children."* Max said.

The lady simply replied **"SPECIAL ONE**, if you look hard enough, you'll notice that your wish has most definitely come true. You have been **blessed with a gift of life**, and this gift is for you letting yourself be **ACCEPTED** by others and other children, and this tells me, that you are just as able as them. So fear not, as your Mummy told you after your first day at Primary school '**You'll be ok!"**

Max smiles and says to the lady, "Thank you, Miss."

34

Hello to everyone, my name is Gavin Clifton. I have lived my entire life in a little village called Pentwynmawr near Newbridge nestled in the heart of South East Wales, UK. I'm blessed to have been for so long surrounded by such loving and caring family and friends, who have treated me as the same as they treat every other person, which I am truly very humbled by. Because of this, I have led pretty much a full and active life to the best of my abilities despite being born with Cerebral Palsy. My life-long dream has been to show others that they can do so too. So, I am so very delighted to do so by writing my true story and also off the back of writing this book, to now be a published Children's Author.

I believe that it is extremely important to showcase both sides of this story, that being someone with a disability, it is acceptable to be different and also to show others that it is ok to be accepting of people who have disabilities and to never judge someone for being different to yourself until you truly get to know them.

I wanted this book to include all of the special qualities of every other Children's Book, to be fun and colourful to read, but still bring both sides of the story together in a unique way, and hopefully, you will have found it does just that, there's so much diversity in the World, we can't let this particular issue be overlooked. I truly hope that this book has been a lot of fun for everyone who has taken time to read it, whilst putting a smile on faces everywhere, keeping in line with the underlying educational and important message behind it.

Thank you for reading 'Max And The Magic Wish', and remember, if you happen to meet a little boy or girl, who is a little different somewhat just like Max is, say 'hello', you may just meet a 'true friend for life.'

Gavin

Printed in Great Britain
by Amazon